English
Progress Papers 3

Patrick Berry and Susan Hamlyn

Schofield & Sims

Introduction

The **English Progress Papers** provide structured activities that increase in difficulty throughout the series, developing your knowledge and skills in English. Use the series to prepare for school entrance examinations, to improve your English knowledge and to practise a range of English skills.

How to use this book

There are six papers in this book. Each contains 85 questions, worth up to 100 marks. A single paper may take between 45 and 75 minutes to complete, and you might need two or more sessions to complete one paper.

For exam preparation, revision and all-round practice, work through the papers in order. Ask an adult helper to mark each paper, correct mistakes and explain where you went wrong. To practise a topic that you find challenging, work through selected activities in order of difficulty using the **Topics chart**, which is free to download from the Schofield & Sims website.

What does each paper contain?

Each paper is divided into three parts. Work carefully through each one and do not rush.

The **English skills** questions focus on key areas of grammar, punctuation and spelling and help you to avoid common mistakes. These questions will also expand your vocabulary, particularly if you incorporate the new words and phrases that you learn in to your own written work.

The multiple-choice **Comprehension** questions are not as easy as they look. Always read both the passage and the question carefully, particularly if all the answer options have some truth in them. One answer is always more accurate than the others, but careful thinking is needed to identify it.

The **Short writing task** is not designed as an extended piece of work and you will be able to complete some tasks in 20 to 30 minutes. Others may inspire you to write for longer – if you need more space, use separate sheets of paper. When working for a test or exam, restrict yourself to 30 minutes' writing, particularly in the last three months before the test. For ideas on how to tackle the different kinds of task, see **Short writing task tips**, which is free to download from the Schofield & Sims website.

Answers

The adult who is helping you will use the pull-out answer booklet to mark your work. If you get some questions wrong, check your answers against the correct answers given. Take time, with a dictionary and/or with an adult, to learn and remember why the answer given is correct. When checking a comprehension question, re-read carefully both the passage and the question and carefully think it through.

Use the **Progress chart** at the back of this book to record your marks and measure progress.

Downloads

Free downloads are available from the Schofield & Sims website (www.schofieldand sims.co.uk/free-downloads) including the resources mentioned above, extra practice material, guidance on alternative spellings, and a glossary of English skills vocabulary.

Published by **Schofield & Sims Ltd**
Dogley Mill, Fenay Bridge, Huddersfield HD8 0NQ, UK
Telephone 01484 607080
www.schofieldandsims.co.uk

First published in 1993
This edition copyright © Schofield & Sims Ltd, 2018

However, the poem 'Before or After' (page 48) remains copyright © Dorothy Nimmo. It is taken from *The Wigbox: New and Selected Poems by Dorothy Nimmo* (Smith|Doorstop Books, 2000), and is reproduced here by kind permission of the publisher.

Authors: **Patrick Berry and Susan Hamlyn**
Patrick Berry and Susan Hamlyn have asserted their moral rights under the Copyright, Designs and Patents Act, 1988, to be identified as the authors of this work.

Grateful thanks to the Head and Year 6 pupils of Notting Hill and Ealing Junior School (GDST) for trialling **English Progress Papers** in their school.

British Library Cataloguing in Publication Data
A catalogue record for this book is available from the British Library.

All rights reserved. No part of this publication may be reproduced, stored in a retrieval system, or transmitted in any form or by any means, electronic, mechanical, photocopying, recording or otherwise, without either the prior permission of the publisher or a licence permitting restricted copying in the United Kingdom issued by the Copyright Licensing Agency Limited, Saffron House, 6–10 Kirby Street, London EC1N 8TS.

Design by **Ledgard Jepson Ltd**

Printed in the UK by **Page Bros (Norwich) Ltd**

ISBN 978 07217 1475 2

Contents

Note for parents, tutors, teachers and other adult helpers

A pull-out answers section (pages A1 to A12) appears in the centre of this book, between pages 26 and 27 (Paper 15). This provides answers to all the **English skills** and **Comprehension** questions, as well as guidelines for marking the **Short writing tasks**. It also gives simple guidance on how best to use this book. Remove the pull-out section before the child begins working through the practice papers.

You may wish the child to have access to a dictionary – either while he or she is working through the papers or after you have marked them. Make a decision on this before the child begins work. You may also give the child some separate sheets of lined paper for continuing the **Short writing task** if needed.

START HERE

Q. 1–60 English skills

MARK

Q. 1–5	Rewrite the text correctly, adding the necessary punctuation.	
punctuation	help cried the injured climber faintly im over here cant you see me	

_____

_____

_____   1–5   5

Q. 6–10

verbs

Add to the sentence a verb that is made from the word shown in capitals.

6   TYPE This good report _____ the quality of your work in general.   6   1

7   SALIVA The hungry man began to _____ when he smelled the onions.   7   1

8   HALF The doctor told me to _____ the amount of food I eat.   8   1

9   IDENTIFICATION You must be able to _____ yourself before entering.   9   1

10   NAUSEA I'd have liked to be a nurse but the sight of blood

_____ me.   10   1

Q. 11–15

homophones

Read the clues, then write the homophones.

11   water from the eyes _____ / rows above rows _____   11   1

12   flat land _____ / carpenter's tool _____   12   1

13   a fruit _____ / a couple _____   13   1

14   rains heavily _____ / holes in the skin _____   14   1

15   let water escape _____ / Welsh emblem _____   15   1

MARK [   ]

English skills

MARK

Q. 16–20	Add to the sentence a noun that is made from the word shown in capitals.		
nouns			
	16 VARIOUS I was amazed at the _____ of her interests.	16	1
	17 FLY The bird's _____ was low and looping.	17	1
	18 SERVE Medieval peasants lived lives of _____.	18	1
	19 COMPOSE Many musical _____ are devised on computers.	19	1
	20 DECEIVE After his _____ I was unable to trust him again.	20	1

Q. 21–25	Three words appear in brackets. Underline the *one* word that is closest in meaning to the word shown in capitals. The word must make sense in the sentence.		
synonyms, word choice			
	21 HELP He asked me to (assist, adept, adapt) him in making the model.	21	1
	22 ATHLETIC Zosia is a very (ample, agile, antic) gymnast.	22	1
	23 KNOWLEDGEABLE The astronomer who gave the talk was a (interesting, scientific, learned) woman.	23	1
	24 TENDED The gardener (nurtured, watched, watered) the seedlings with great care and skill.	24	1
	25 DETECTIVE Sherlock Holmes was a very clever (inspector, sleuth, officer).	25	1

Q. 26–30	Write down the meaning of the phrase.		
word meanings			
	26 rough and ready _____	26	1
	27 spick and span _____	27	1
	28 kith and kin _____	28	1
	29 all and sundry _____	29	1
	30 null and void _____	30	1

MARK

English skills

MARK

Q. 31–35	Add the *one* missing word, using the Latin or Greek root as a clue.	
word meanings	**31** *Aqua* means *water*. A bridge carrying water is an _____.	31 [ ] 1
	32 *Centum* means a *hundred*. A hundred years is a _____.	32 [ ] 1
	33 *Navis* means *ship*. A fleet of ships is a _____.	33 [ ] 1
	34 *Octo* means *eight*. A creature with eight tentacles is an _____.	34 [ ] 1
	35 *Decimus* means *tenth*. To kill every tenth person in a group is to _____ that group.	35 [ ] 1

Q. 36–40	Unscramble the anagram to fit the meaning given.	
anagrams	**36** NOT PAM H (a ghost) _____	36 [ ] 1
	37 FLING IN BAR ZONE (a huge fire [two words]) _____	37 [ ] 1
	38 ALANS ARMED (a lizard-like creature) _____	38 [ ] 1
	39 CRIED (a drink made of apples) _____	39 [ ] 1
	40 RED RUM (kill) _____	40 [ ] 1

Q. 41–45	In each sentence write an adjective formed from the word shown in capitals.	
adjectives	**41** LOGIC There doesn't appear to be a _____ explanation.	41 [ ] 1
	42 INFORM It was an _____ talk and I learned a lot from it.	42 [ ] 1
	43 DELIRIUM She was _____ with joy when she heard the news.	43 [ ] 1
	44 DESPOT The _____ ruler treated his subjects cruelly.	44 [ ] 1
	45 LOATHE A _____ monster emerged from the swamp.	45 [ ] 1

MARK [   ]

English skills   MARK

Q. 46–50 word choice	Put the word in the sentence where it makes the best sense. veracity, voracity, loquacious, eloquent, reticent	
	46 Unlike the others, that _____ child never stops talking!	46 1
	47 We were all moved by her _____ and moving speech.	47 1
	48 We were sceptical and doubted the _____ of their story.	48 1
	49 The _____ woman contributes nothing to the discussion.	49 1
	50 The giant devoured the sailors with great _____.	50 1

Q. 51–55 homonyms	Write the one word that has both meanings.	
	51 a mark with a meaning / to write one's signature _____	51 1
	52 a blood-sucking mite / the noise of a watch _____	52 1
	53 the body from waist to knees when sitting / once round a race track _____	53 1
	54 sound made by a hound / an inlet of the sea _____	54 1
	55 number problem in maths / total _____	55 1

Q. 56–60 prefixes, spelling	The prefix quad means four. Fill in the missing letters to make the word.	
	56 A figure with four sides is a quad _ _ _ _ _ _ _ _ _.	56 1
	57 A creature with four legs is a quad _ _ _ _ _.	57 1
	58 If you multiply a number by four you quad _ _ _ _ _ it.	58 1
	59 Four babies born at once to the same mother are called quad _ _ _ _ _ _ s.	59 1
	60 One of four equal parts of a circle is called a quad _ _ _ _.	60 1

MARK [   ]

ENGLISH SKILLS SUB-TOTAL [   ] 60

Q. 61–75 Comprehension

MARK

Read this passage carefully.

Zofia Makes her Mark

"They won't give you any trouble," Andy assured her. "All they care about is getting to the top of the league. And another few wins will make that a realistic prospect."

Zofia bounced the ball and balanced it on the tip of her boot.
"Thanks," she said. "I can't wait to get on with it."

5   "The only one who might give you a bit of stick is Rufus," continued Andy. "He's seen you play, he knows what you've achieved but he can't get his head round a woman coach."
"I'm going to have to prove myself?"
"I think so."
"That's OK by me."

10   Andy led her out on to the pitch, where the men were warming up, practising tackles. Andy blew his whistle and they all stopped and cantered over to where he and Zofia waited.

Andy pointed to the bandaged knee of Ashley Bennett, who was their most successful striker.
"What's that all about?"
Ashley looked a bit shame-faced.

15   "I'm sorry, Andy. I . . . er . . . fell off my motor bike. It's not broken but it's a bit of a mess."
"Can I see?" asked Zofia.
Ashley looked at Andy.
"She's the boss," responded Andy.
"Come inside a minute," said Zofia, leading Ashley back to the locker room.

20   The players looked at each other anxiously.
"Carry on warming up," instructed Andy – and the men spread back over the field, knocking the ball back and forth, keeping an eye on the door into the sports centre.

It was a good 10 minutes before Zofia returned – alone. The men all ran back.
"I've sent him home," she said. "That knee's going to need three weeks' rest."

25   "You are not serious!" exclaimed Rufus. "We're playing City on Saturday and we've got no chance without Ash!"
"I'm serious," replied Zofia. "Now – let's get going."
Rufus didn't move.

Now read these questions. You have a choice of four answers
to each question. Choose the *one* answer you think the best.
Draw a line in the box next to its letter, like this.

A ⊟

61   The passage starts in the middle of a conversation. Which of the following do you think Zofia said immediately before Andy's first words in lines 1 and 2?

A "I really can't wait to meet them. They're such a brilliant team!"   A ☐

B "I can't see why a woman shouldn't manage a men's team. Plenty of men train women."   B ☐

C "I'm dead nervous. I just hope we can work together."   C ☐

D "Thanks for giving me the job. I'm really looking forward to it."   D ☐   61   2

MARK ☐

Comprehension
MARK

62 Which phrase below best completes this sentence?

Andy thinks that the team has _____ of winning the league.

A a decent chance

B no chance at all

C a small chance

D a certainty

62   2

63 Which word or phrase best completes this sentence?

Andy is anticipating that Rufus might be difficult with Zofia _____
her impressive reputation.

A despite

B because of

C although

D except for

63   2

64 The word 'cantered' (line 11) is more usually used of which of the following?

A cattle

B horses

C racing cars

D runners

64   2

65 How many nouns, verbs and adjectives are used in this sentence?

Andy pointed to the bandaged knee of Ashley, who was their most
successful striker.

A four nouns, one verb, two adjectives

B three nouns, two verbs, no adjectives

C two nouns, one verb, one adjective

D four nouns, two verbs, two adjectives

65   2

66 'Ashley looked a bit shame-faced' (line 14). Which of the following words means
the same as 'shame-faced'?

A disappointed

B furious

C agonised

D embarrassed

66   2

67 '"Come inside a minute," said Zofia, leading Ashley back to the locker room' (line 19).
What quality do you think Zofia is demonstrating at this point in the story?

A authority

B bossiness

C nosiness

D worry

67   2

MARK

Comprehension   MARK

68 Which word best describes the atmosphere on the field while Zofia and Ashley are in the locker room?

    A skilful   A ☐

    B focused   B ☐

    C tense   C ☐

    D enthusiastic   D ☐   68 ☐ 2

69 '"You are not serious!" exclaimed Rufus. "We're playing City on Saturday and we've got no chance without Ash!"' (lines 25–26). How would you describe Rufus's reaction?

    A challenging   A ☐

    B obstructive   B ☐

    C distraught   C ☐

    D livid   D ☐   69 ☐ 2

70 Which one of the following have we reached at the end of the passage?

    A a stand-to   A ☐

    B a stand-up   B ☐

    C a stand-off   C ☐

    D a stand-in   D ☐   70 ☐ 2

71 Zofia has two major tasks in this passage: to help the team win the league and to make them accept her as manager. Which of the following qualities – in addition to footballing expertise – do you think she will need the most?

    A courage   A ☐

    B confidence   B ☐

    C consistency   C ☐

    D calm   D ☐   71 ☐ 2

Find the spelling mistake. Underline it and write the box letter at the end of the line.

72   Prowess in sport   is largely dependent   on consistent   practise.

           A   B   C   D   ☐   72 ☐ 2

73   Olympian athletes   train religiously and   with compleet   dedication.

           A   B   C   D   ☐   73 ☐ 2

74   Trainers of professional   sportsmen and women   mesure their   progress closely.

           A   B   C   D   ☐   74 ☐ 2

75   Wieght training   and muscle building   are significant in   attaining proficiency.

           A   B   C   D   ☐   75 ☐ 2

MARK ☐

COMPREHENSION SUB-TOTAL ☐ 30

Q. 76–85 Short writing task

MARK

Write for 20–30 minutes on *one* of the following. Continue on a separate sheet if you need to.

a) Continue the story 'Zofia Makes her Mark' from where it leaves off.

b) Imagine you are Ashley. Write your blog entry for that day.

c) These days most jobs are open to men and women equally. Prepare a speech for a class discussion in which you argue *either* for *or* against the idea that there should be no restrictions as to who does any particular job.

END OF TEST

SHORT WRITING TASK SUB-TOTAL	10
English skills sub-total (from page 7)	60
Comprehension sub-total (from page 10)	30
Short writing task sub-total (from this page)	10
PAPER 13 TOTAL MARK	100

START HERE

Q. 1–60 English skills

MARK

Q. 1–5 punctuation	Rewrite the text correctly, adding the necessary punctuation.		

that was an interesting story said mrs patel smiling could you put in some pictures now but im rubbish at drawing replied henry

_____

_____

_____

1–5   5

Q. 6–10 word meanings, synonyms	Underline the *one* word that is closest in meaning to the word shown in capitals.

6   NEGLIGENCE   exhibition, omelette, carelessness, nightwear   6 ☐ 1

7   QUANDARY   dilemma, quagmire, attribute, laundry   7 ☐ 1

8   PYROMANIAC   sadist, fanatic, madman, arsonist   8 ☐ 1

9   ROTUND   eatable, rotten, round, exciting   9 ☐ 1

10   INANE   awkward, definite, sensible, senseless   10 ☐ 1

Q. 11–15 prefixes	Put the prefix in the word where it makes the best sense.

con, pro, dis, anti, super

11   You have written too much. Can you _____dense it?   11 ☐ 1

12   For my hay fever I use an _____histamine inhaler.   12 ☐ 1

13   I adore ghost stories and all things _____natural.   13 ☐ 1

14   A _____fusion of flowers filled the overgrown garden.   14 ☐ 1

15   He looked at the burnt pizza with a _____approving frown.   15 ☐ 1

MARK ☐

English skills

MARK

Q. 16–20 nouns	Add to the sentence a noun that is made from the word shown in capitals.		
	16 FESTIVE A birthday is usually a time for celebration and _____.	16	1
	17 CONTRAVENE Any _____ of the law will be taken seriously.	17	1
	18 CONTINUE The _____ of having the same teacher all year is good.	18	1
	19 CONVALESCE After her operation, Rupa's _____ took months.	19	1
	20 DRAMATIC The play was written by a well-known _____.	20	1

Q. 21–25 indirect to direct speech	Change the sentence from indirect to direct speech.		
	21 Shabana remarked that she had not heard the post arrive that day. _____	21	1
	22 Louis asked the shop assistant the price of the cakes. _____	22	1
	23 Everybody in the class was asked by the teacher to stand up. _____	23	1
	24 The mechanic shouted to his apprentice for some help. _____	24	1
	25 The Captain warned us that a severe storm was on its way. _____	25	1

Q. 26–30 adjectives	Add to the sentence an adjective that is made from the word shown in capitals.		
	26 ENIGMA He responded to my question with an _____ smile.	26	1
	27 NEUROSIS My gran becomes _____ if I don't wash before eating.	27	1
	28 CLARITY "You mustn't talk to strangers," said Mum. "I hope that is _____."	28	1
	29 RHYTHM The dancers moved to the _____ beat of the music.	29	1
	30 DOGMA Mr Hughes can be _____ and unwilling to hear others' opinions.	30	1

MARK

English skills

MARK

Q. 31–35 prefixes, spelling	The prefix *contra* or *contro* means *against*. Fill in the missing letters to make a word.	

31 If you argue against somebody you contra __ __ __ __ him or her.

31 ☐ 1

32 A system for directing traffic in the opposite direction from normal is a contra __ __ __ __.

32 ☐ 1

33 A question about which there are differing opinions is contro __ __ __ __ __ __ __ .

33 ☐ 1

34 Another word for opposite is contra __ __.

34 ☐ 1

35 Goods smuggled into a country against the law are called contra __ __ __ __.

35 ☐ 1

Q. 36–40 word meanings, suffixes	Complete the definition of the *ology*.

36 Ophthalmology is the study of _____.

36 ☐ 1

37 Zoology is the study of _____.

37 ☐ 1

38 Cardiology is the study of _____.

38 ☐ 1

39 Neurology is the study of _____.

39 ☐ 1

40 Psychology is the study of _____.

40 ☐ 1

Q. 41–45 word choice	Use the form of the verbs *lie* or *lay* that completes the sentence correctly.

41 He was _____ down on the floor.

41 ☐ 1

42 The rubbish had _____ there for weeks.

42 ☐ 1

43 My sister _____ the table.

43 ☐ 1

44 Which hen has _____ the most eggs?

44 ☐ 1

45 Very gently, they _____ down the injured boy.

45 ☐ 1

MARK ☐

English skills

MARK

Q. 46–50

unscramble sentences

Unscramble the sentence so that it makes sense. Write the sentence on the line. Include capital letters and punctuation as needed.

46 lasagne dinner have please we for could

_____

46   1

47 a our in a disneyland disaster was of holiday bit

_____

47   1

48 hibernate dreams must who very have long animals

_____

48   1

49 because the late strike started rehearsal of the

_____

49   1

50 chocolate be were less would I delicious slimmer if

_____

50   1

Q. 51–55

word choice

Put the word in the sentence where it makes the best sense. You will need to use one of the words twice.

    implement, compliment, complement, competent

51 The ship set sail with a full _____ of sailors.

51   1

52 We must _____ the proposals made by the council.

52   1

53 A trowel is an _____ used by a builder.

53   1

54 This pilot is extremely _____ so I know we are safe.

54   1

55 "I must _____ you," said the head, "on your good work."

55   1

Q. 56–60

spelling

Read the clue. Fill in the missing letters to make the word.

56 information and learning   k _ _ _ _ _ _ _ e

56   1

57 on the roof, the television needs it   a _ _ _ _ _ _

57   1

58 place to stay – for example, in a hotel   a _ _ _ _ _ _ _ _ _ _ n

58   1

59 a crunchy cookie   b _ _ _ _ _ t

59   1

60 employment or profession   b _ _ _ _ _ _ s

60   1

MARK

ENGLISH SKILLS SUB-TOTAL   60

Q. 61–75 Comprehension

MARK

Read this passage carefully.

RISTORANTE CLAUDIA

Our restaurant critic, Ivor Plate, reviews this family pizzeria and restaurant.
Proprietor: Claudia Minelli. Seats 46.

Typical menu

Pizzas:

- **Pizza Margarita Classic** – simplest and most authentic pizza – with our own homemade tomato pesto, olive oil
5 and real Italian mozzarella cheese
- **Pizza Quattro Stagione** – Four Seasons pizza with artichokes, prosciutto and cooked ham, pepperoni and fresh mushrooms on a crispy tomato and mozzarella base
10 • **Pizza Salsiccia** – white pizza with Sicilian sausage meat, broccoli, mozzarella, fresh cream, garlic, olive oil and fresh chilli
- **Pizza Tirolese** – pizza from northern Italy with Tirolese Speck (smoked ham from the mountains), fresh
15 mushrooms, mozzarella and a drizzle of natural olive oil

Mains:

- **Italian roast chicken** – in lemon and rosemary with olive oil potatoes, fresh vegetables in season
- **Lamb's liver in a herb crust** – with French fries and
20 buttery mash, fresh vegetables in season
- **Risotto primavera** – Arborio rice with a selection of spring vegetables and parmesan cheese
- **Ravioli classic** – cheese-filled pasta in a deliciously rich tomato sauce with cream

25 **Review**

The food comes quickly in Claudia's restaurant – almost too quickly. You wonder whether it's been cooked, kept warm and is waiting hopefully for someone to order it. The service is friendly but a bit slapdash – it seems a matter 30 of luck whether you get what you order – but everyone smiles and seems to care that you enjoy your food. The wine list is predictable but not intimidating and some of the desserts, while not being exactly imaginative, hit the spot and make the visit worthwhile – we recommend 35 the homemade tarts, the tiramisu and the chocolate ice-cream cake. Not the place for a lovers' quiet meal – the candlelight is decidedly prone to the draughts from the door and the crashing from the kitchen can be alarming – but a good place for a cheerful, inexpensive midweek family meal.

Now read these questions. You have a choice of four answers to each question. Choose the *one* answer you think the best. Draw a line in the box next to its letter, like this.

A ▭

61 How many couples could eat simultaneously at the Ristorante Claudia?

- A 13
- B 23
- C 18
- D 24

61 ☐ 2

62 How many vegetables are mentioned specifically in the pizza menu only?
Mushrooms, tomatoes, chilli, garlic and olives are *not* vegetables.

- A four
- B five
- C six
- D two

62 ☐ 2

MARK ☐

Comprehension

63 Which of the following are listed?

- A a sample of the dishes on the menu
- B characteristic dishes on the menu
- C delicious dishes on the menu
- D memorable dishes on the menu

A ☐
B ☐
C ☐
D ☐

63   2

64 Which of the following could a vegetarian eat?

- A all the pizzas and one of the mains on the menu
- B three of the pizzas and none of the mains on the menu
- C none of the pizzas and two of the mains on the menu
- D one of the pizzas and two of the mains on the menu

A ☐
B ☐
C ☐
D ☐

64   2

65 What does Ivor Plate feel about the time that he has to wait for his food?

- A He feels that he has to wait too long.
- B He feels that he has to wait a surprisingly short time.
- C The wait makes him feel impatient.
- D He feels that he does not have to wait long enough.

A ☐
B ☐
C ☐
D ☐

65   2

66 What is the meaning of the word 'slapdash' (line 29)?

- A clumsy
- B rude
- C careless
- D rough

A ☐
B ☐
C ☐
D ☐

66   2

67 How does Ivor Plate feel about the waiting staff?

- A that they want the customers to like the meal
- B that they don't care at all about the customers
- C that they are kind but bored
- D that they are very lucky

A ☐
B ☐
C ☐
D ☐

67   2

68 What does Ivor Plate say about the wine list?

- A that it is disappointing
- B that it has no surprises
- C that it is frightening
- D that it is expensive

A ☐
B ☐
C ☐
D ☐

68   2

69 Ivor Plate says that the desserts 'while not being exactly imaginative, hit the spot' (lines 33–34). What does he mean by this?

- A that the puddings are expensive and nasty
- B that although the puddings are small they are delicious
- C that although the puddings are unexciting they taste good
- D that the puddings are surprising and wake you up

A ☐
B ☐
C ☐
D ☐

69   2

MARK ☐

Comprehension

MARK

70 Which of the following words best describes the atmosphere in Ristorante Claudia?

  A cold

  B luxurious

  C family-friendly

  D posh

A ☐

B ☐

C ☐

D ☐

70   2

71 What does Ivor Plate suggest about three of the desserts (lines 32–36)?

  A that they are delicious

  B that they are awful

  C that they justify going to the restaurant

  D that they are homemade

A ☐

B ☐

C ☐

D ☐

71   2

72 Choose the most appropriate word from the list to fill the gap.

The _____ appearance of the food in Ristorante Claudia surprised Ivor Plate.

  A casual

  B rapid

  C tired

  D messy

A ☐

B ☐

C ☐

D ☐

72   2

73 Lines 36–39 suggest that Ristorante Claudia is all but one of the following. Identify the word that does *not* apply.

  A draughty

  B romantic

  C cheerful

  D noisy

A ☐

B ☐

C ☐

D ☐

73   2

74 We are told that the meals at Ristorante Claudia are 'inexpensive' (line 39) – that is, the opposite of 'expensive'. Which *one* of the prefixes below goes in front of *all* the words in this list to make their opposites?

   natural, intelligent, savoury, promising

  A in

  B un

  C dis

  D mis

A ☐

B ☐

C ☐

D ☐

74   2

75 Which *one* of the following phrases do you feel best describes Ivor Plate's review?

  A straightforward and factual

  B highly critical

  C appreciative but gently humorous

  D unfair and ungenerous

A ☐

B ☐

C ☐

D ☐

75   2

MARK ☐

COMPREHENSION SUB-TOTAL ☐ 30

Q. 76–85 Short writing task

MARK

Write for 20–30 minutes on *one* of the following. Continue on a separate sheet if you need to.

a) The Day We Went Out to Eat

b) Think of a dish or a meal that you know well and like. Write detailed instructions on how to make it. Try to include ingredients and quantities – you can guess at these if necessary!

c) There are professional critics not only of restaurants but also of films, books, music, dance and theatrical productions. Would you like to do one of these jobs? Say which you would choose and how you would approach the job.

END OF TEST

	MARK
SHORT WRITING TASK SUB-TOTAL	10
English skills sub-total (from page 15)	60
Comprehension sub-total (from page 18)	30
Short writing task sub-total (from this page)	10
PAPER 14 TOTAL MARK	100

START HERE

Q. 1–60 English skills

MARK

Q. 1–5 punctuation	Rewrite the sentence correctly, adding the necessary punctuation.	
	venita a brilliant tennis player won her match though sadly she fell straining her wrist and breaking her mums racquet	
	_____	
	_____	
	_____	**1–5** 5

Q. 6–10 verbs	Add to the sentence a verb that is made from the word shown in capitals.	
	6 FURY "That man's driving _____ me!" said Mum, crossly.	**6** 1
	7 PORTENT "What does this sign _____ ?" he asked.	**7** 1
	8 BATH It is said that Queen Elizabeth I _____ only once a year.	**8** 1
	9 CIRCLE The army _____ the enemy before attacking.	**9** 1
	10 COMPANY Charlotte asked Ajit to _____ her to the bus stop.	**10** 1

Q. 11–15 grammar	Write out the sentence, correcting any errors.	
	11 She didn't speak very clear.	
	_____	**11** 1
	12 The teacher learned him many facts.	
	_____	**12** 1
	13 Me and my friend went shopping.	
	_____	**13** 1
	14 He was so helpful I could of hugged him.	
	_____	**14** 1
	15 My brother lay the table for tea.	
	_____	**15** 1

MARK [ ]

Schofield & Sims • **English Progress Papers 3**

English skills   MARK

Q. 16–20	Write the missing parts of speech of the word shown in capitals.					
parts of speech, nouns, adjectives, adverbs, verbs		**NOUN**	**ADJECTIVE**	**ADVERB**	**VERB**	
	Example:	HEALTH	_healthy_	_healthily_	_heal_	
	16	BEAUTY	_____	_____	_____	16 1
	17	SECRET	_____	_____	_____	17 1
	18	WEAKNESS	_____	_____	_____	18 1
	19	DARKNESS	_____	_____	_____	19 1
	20	GLORY	_____	_____	_____	20 1

Q. 21–25	Unscramble the sentence so that it makes sense. Write the sentence on the line. Include capital letters and punctuation as needed.	
unscramble sentences	21 exciting treasure find buried would very to be it	
	_____	21 1
	22 girl little called have parents adopted a alice joe's	
	_____	22 1
	23 the northern grow all of battlefields france poppies over	
	_____	23 1
	24 best invented Lego ever toy the think i is	
	_____	24 1
	25 i friend love but prefers my cats dogs	
	_____	25 1

Q. 26–30	Read the clue. Fill in the missing letters to make the word.	
word meanings	26 a person who chooses not to eat meat v _ _ _ _ _ _ _ _ _	26 1
	27 the study of plants b _ _ _ _ _	27 1
	28 able to live in water or on land a _ _ _ _ _ _ _ _ _	28 1
	29 catches fire easily i _ _ _ _ _ _ _ _ _	29 1
	30 it counteracts poison a _ _ _ _ _ _ _	30 1

MARK

English skills   MARK

Q. 31–35	Underline the *one* word on the right that belongs with the three on the left.	
word groups (by meaning)	**31** road, street, avenue / lane, estate, garden, home	**31** ☐ 1
	32 proverb, saying, adage / minim, maxim, quaver, crochet	**32** ☐ 1
	33 drill, hammer, screwdriver / car, train, chisel, boat	**33** ☐ 1
	34 strapping, strong, sturdy / robust, bankrupt, stiff, tall	**34** ☐ 1
	35 fifth, twelfth, eighth / twenty, second, dozen, fourteen	**35** ☐ 1

Q. 36–40	The prefix *oct* or *octo* means *eight*. Read the clue. Fill in the missing letters to make the word.	
prefixes, spelling	**36** figure with eight sides and angles oct _ _ _ _	**36** ☐ 1
	37 group of eight musicians oct _ _	**37** ☐ 1
	38 eighth month in the Roman calendar Oct _ _ _ _	**38** ☐ 1
	39 800th anniversary oct _ _ _ _ _ _ _ _ _	**39** ☐ 1
	40 eight consecutive musical notes oct _ _ _	**40** ☐ 1

Q. 41–45	Underline the *one* word that is closest in meaning to the word shown in capitals.	
word meanings, synonyms	**41** PANACEA fright, remedy, utensil, company	**41** ☐ 1
	42 PROCRASTINATE mumble, fascinate, tremble, delay	**42** ☐ 1
	43 TRUCULENT aggressive, honest, kind, foolish	**43** ☐ 1
	44 PRIMARY first, young, small, easy	**44** ☐ 1
	45 ASSASSIN sofa, shrub, killer, knife	**45** ☐ 1

MARK ☐

English skills   MARK

Q. 46–50	To which part of the orchestra do the instruments belong? Write the word on the line.		
word groups (by meaning)	brass, strings, keyboards, percussion, woodwind		

46 drums and cymbals   _____   46 1

47 flutes and clarinets   _____   47 1

48 violins and cellos   _____   48 1

49 trumpets and horns   _____   49 1

50 organ and synthesiser   _____   50 1

Q. 51–55

nouns

Add to the sentence a noun that is made from the word shown in capitals.

51 PERSPIRE After a gruelling race, _____ dripped from my body.   51 1

52 FRAGRANT A wonderful _____ came from the herb garden.   52 1

53 DROWSY As I lay down, a feeling of _____ came over me.   53 1

54 ALERT Thanks to the watchman's _____ the fire was seen in time.   54 1

55 HARASS "I don't need all this _____ ," said John.   55 1

Q. 56–60

word choice

Two words appear in brackets. Underline the *one* word that completes the sentence correctly.

56 The plant food had a weird (affect/effect) on my hydrangea.   56 1

57 Could you (affect/effect) an escape if I gave you a rope ladder?   57 1

58 The new glasses (affected/effected) my eyesight for the better.   58 1

59 If I play my music, will it (affect/effect) your concentration?   59 1

60 The medicine was very (affective/effective).   60 1

MARK

ENGLISH SKILLS SUB-TOTAL   60

Q. 61–75 Comprehension

MARK

Read this passage carefully.

The Day that Changed my Summer

Amber watches her dad get ready to go away.

I had seen it so often before. Ever since I was a toddler, I'd got used to the other members of the band arriving, the heaving into the van and the trailer of keyboard, lengths of electric cable, guitars in their cases, stands, Luke's drums and sticks, boxes of CDs that they hoped to return without, and endless bits of tackle I couldn't identify then but got to know later. Each member of the band brought a rucksack
5 with all the clothes they would wear on the tour. I never understood how they managed with so little, but it made every kind of sense. Even with the trailer they were crammed into the van – four of them plus Jodie the Roadie – and the rucksacks were heaped up behind them, too high for Dad – who always drove – to see out of the rear window.

I had always hated it – while also being excited and full of questions. Where would they spend the first
10 night? Were all the venues fully booked already? What was the biggest audience they could get? How many CDs were they taking – how many of the latest one and how many of the older ones? Did they have the playlist already planned for each gig or would they decide on the way? And I loved it too – the gentle joking, the quiet understanding they shared, the age-old friendships.

But everything changed that day. School had just broken up and a summer without Dad at home looked
15 pretty bleak. The van was half packed, they were just waiting for Jodie who was never normally late. Then Dad's mobile burped. "Hi," he said and then turned down the garden path. With the traffic snoring past, we couldn't hear what he was saying. The others carried on loading up the van but I could see from Dad's shoulders that all was not well. He quickly came back up the path, pushing his mobile into his back pocket.
20 "Jodie's not coming," he said. "Her dad's had a heart attack. She's got to stay with her mum."
Luke sat on the garden wall.
"That's us properly messed up, then," he said. "We can't go without a roadie."
There was silence. Then Dad looked at me.
"You've got five minutes to pack a bag," he said.

Now read these questions. You have a choice of four answers
to each question. Choose the *one* answer you think the best.
Draw a line in the box next to its letter, like this.

A �

61 Which phrase best completes this sentence?

Amber's dad is preparing to go on a tour with _____.

A his friends

B his tackle

C his band

D his family

61 ☐ 2

62 Which of the following would *not* be an appropriate word for what they are packing into the van?

A gear

B kit

C machinery

D equipment

62 ☐ 2

MARK ☐

Comprehension

MARK

63 What did the band members bring with them in the way of clothes?

A very few clothes
B several changes of clothes
C clothes for each occasion
D very thin clothes

A ☐
B ☐
C ☐
D ☐

63   2

64 The word 'roadie' (lines 7 and 22) is short for 'road manager'. Which of the following would *not* be part of a roadie's role?

A liaising with the venues
B managing bookings
C playing the bass in each concert
D being responsible for the technical side of gigs

A ☐
B ☐
C ☐
D ☐

64   2

65 Which of the following sentences best describes Amber's feelings in the second paragraph?

A She was excited and curious.
B She hated them getting ready to go.
C She had mixed feelings.
D She loved every part of it.

A ☐
B ☐
C ☐
D ☐

65   2

66 What does line 13 suggest about the band members?

A that they have known each other a long time
B that they don't say much
C that they are very old now
D that they are very funny

A ☐
B ☐
C ☐
D ☐

66   2

67 Which of the following statements is true?

A Amber is looking forward to the school holidays.
B Amber has had a row with a friend.
C Amber is looking forward to having her home to herself.
D Amber is not looking forward to the summer.

A ☐
B ☐
C ☐
D ☐

67   2

68 How does Amber know that there is a problem, even before Dad tells them the news?

A Dad takes the mobile away for a private conversation.
B Dad's shoulders are hunching up.
C Dad tucks the mobile away before he comes back.
D The conversation is very short.

A ☐
B ☐
C ☐
D ☐

68   2

69 Which word best describes Luke's response?

A defeatist
B disgusted
C disapproving
D decisive

A ☐
B ☐
C ☐
D ☐

69   2

MARK ☐

Comprehension

MARK

70 How does the passage end?

A humorously

B dramatically

C scarily

D conversationally

A
B
C
D

70 ☐ 2

71 In the next five minutes after the events described in the passage have taken place, Amber frantically packs a bag. She is feeling excited. Which word best describes the other feelings that she probably has?

A apprehensive

B appreciative

C appalled

D appraised

A
B
C
D

71 ☐ 2

72 While on the road, Luke starts to teach Amber some of the jobs she'll be doing. Which of the following words do you think best describes how Amber will write down notes on what Luke tells her?

A automatically

B aggressively

C assiduously

D abrasively

A
B
C
D

72 ☐ 2

73 Which word best completes this sentence?

Amber feels thrilled but also anxious about the _____ of responsibility she is bearing.

A size

B importance

C sense

D burden

A
B
C
D

73 ☐ 2

74 Just before the first concert, the stage lights fuse. Which of these people does Amber need to talk to?

A the lighting designer

B the electrician

C the caretaker

D the switchboard operator

A
B
C
D

74 ☐ 2

75 The tour goes brilliantly and Amber is very relieved. At the end of the tour, the band has a new song. Which of these might be the best title for the song?

A Amazing Amber

B Bye Bye Jodie

C Roadie Ran Out

D Lights Out!

A
B
C
D

75 ☐ 2

MARK ☐

COMPREHENSION SUB-TOTAL ☐ 30

English
Progress Papers 3
Answers

Schofield&Sims

English Progress Papers 3

Notes for parents, tutors, teachers and other helpers

This pull-out book contains correct answers to all the questions in **English Progress Papers 3**, and is designed to assist you, the adult helper, as you mark the child's work. Once the child has become accustomed to the method of working, you may wish to give him or her direct access to this pull-out section.

When marking, write the number of marks achieved in the tinted column on the far right of the question page. The number to the right of the white mark box indicates the maximum mark available for that question. Sub-total boxes at the foot of each page will help you to add marks quickly. You can then fill in the total marks at the end of the paper. Here you can record separately the child's score in each of the three parts of the paper. The total score is out of 100 and therefore yields a percentage result. The child's progress can be recorded using the **Progress chart** on page 52.

Each paper is divided into three sections, as follows.

	Number of questions	Total marks available	Approximate time available
English skills	60	60	10–20 minutes
Comprehension	15	30	15–25 minutes
Short writing task	The child chooses and completes one of three tasks, for which 10 marks may be gained.	10	20–30 minutes
Totals	**85 questions**	**100 marks**	**45–75 minutes**

English skills (60 questions, worth a total of 60 marks)

This first section comprises 12 groups of five brief questions. In **English Progress Papers 3**, you can expect children to take between 10 and 20 minutes to complete it. Each group of questions tests a particular area of literacy skill or knowledge. Most of the questions in this first section have right or wrong answers (for example, the adjective made from the noun *glory* is *glorious*). However, some do not and a range of answers is possible. If the question asks, for example, for a sentence to be changed from indirect to direct speech then some variation from the suggested answer is acceptable. You must make your own judgement concerning these questions.

The questions in this section are worth one mark if answered correctly. The only exception is the somewhat longer punctuation question at the start of each paper, which is allocated a maximum of five marks. In all questions like these, where the right answer includes several different elements, give full marks only if the response is completely correct and covers all the constituent parts.

Some English words can be spelt correctly in more than one way. For a free download providing notes and guidance on alternative spellings, visit the Schofield & Sims website.

Comprehension (15 questions, worth a total of 30 marks)

The second section offers passages for comprehension followed by 15 multiple-choice questions, each with a choice of four possible answers – only one of which should be chosen. The Comprehension section in this book should take children between 15 and 25 minutes to answer. The questions vary in difficulty, but you should tell the child to assume that they are more difficult than they might at first appear. Encourage the child to read carefully both the passage and the question before answering. Sometimes, the distinction between several of the possible answers offered is subtle: care and re-reading of both the passage and the question may be needed before the choice is made.

A correctly answered Comprehension question is worth two marks. This reflects the importance of these questions, which test understanding of the passage as well as grammar and spelling.

Short writing task (worth a total of 10 marks)

The third section allows the child between 20 and 30 minutes to write a brief composition on one of three topics. Space is available for the piece of writing to be written on the page, directly below the list of topics. However, the child may need an extra sheet of paper on which to continue, so be sure to have some available.

Marking a child's composition is not an exact science, but generally speaking you should give credit for strengths and deduct marks for deficiencies. The guidelines below will help you to give the child's writing a mark out of 10. Please bear in mind that, at this level, it should not be impossible for a lively and accurately written piece to gain full marks.

Where an essay title is provided, this may be interpreted exactly as the child wishes. For example, the title 'A Very Old Building' (Paper 17, option a), could prompt the child to write a description of a real building or a completely fictional story. In total, this series provides 54 essay topics, requiring a range of writing skills and styles as listed opposite, used for a variety of purposes and aimed at different readers. Help the child to understand that not all writing is the same: they would not write a thank-you letter to their grandparents in the same style as a speech to be read out in class or a story for a younger child.

Give credit for:	Deduct marks for:
• writing in a style appropriate to the task and audience (see table opposite)	• inappropriate style – for example, too formal or informal for purpose and/or audience (see table opposite)
• correct spelling and punctuation, legible handwriting	• poor spelling and/or illegibility
• appropriate use of paragraphing and the setting out of dialogue	• inadequate or misplaced punctuation, paragraphing, use of capital letters
• correct grammar (allow some leeway for, for example, colloquial conversation, especially if it is expressive of individual character)	• writing that loses its way, is irrelevant to the title, doesn't make sense or is repetitive
• consistency within the piece of writing in the use of verb tenses	• inconsistent use of verb tenses – moving from past to present or vice versa
• use of interesting, varied and lively vocabulary	• inconsistent narrative approach – for example, changing from third person to first person or changing tenses mid-narrative
• narrative, descriptive or explicatory flair – for example, in holding the reader's attention, story twists, imaginative use of language	• a sense that the writer is not in control and is either struggling to write enough or struggling to contain an idea that is too big for the time allowed
• an overall sense of control and confidence	

The table opposite highlights different aspects of style – arranged by task type and designed to help you as you mark different types of writing. Discourage the child from always choosing the 'story' option. The experience of tackling the varied writing tasks provided in this series will give the child the skills and confidence to write well – not just in English tests but in all other aspects of study and life where writing matters.

Task type	Book 3	
Story writing • A 30-minute time limit does not allow for a large cast or for several changes of place and day. The story will work best if the action happens all in one go, in one location and with only a few participants. • It is best for the child to avoid a long introduction, unless it is vital to the story. Award an extra mark if the child plunges straight into the story. This is particularly important, of course, if the child has been asked to continue the story where it left off or to write from a particular character's viewpoint. • Even bearing in mind these limitations, you may still find pace, dialogue and description that helps you to imagine the events, setting and atmosphere.	Paper 13a) Paper 14a) Paper 15a)	Paper 16a) Paper 17a) Paper 18a)
Concise description • Look for evidence that the child has taken account of the intended audience for the piece of writing and adjusted his or her style accordingly. • For example, if the piece of writing requested is for a website or magazine, look for a concise style that will keep the attention of readers: watch out for too much detail, particularly any facts that are irrelevant to the audience.	Paper 13b) Paper 14a) Paper 15a)	Paper 17c)
Detailed description • Where a full description is required, give marks for clearly imagined and carefully crafted prose. • Look for descriptions that give a strong sense of the person, place or thing.		Paper 16c) Paper 17a) Paper 18a) Paper 18c)
Instructions, persuasive writing and explanations • Clarity of thinking makes for clarity of expression. Before the child starts writing, he or she needs first to identify the purpose of the piece of writing. • *Instructions* need to be simple, correctly ordered and straightforward. • *Writing that aims to persuade or to influence* should avoid nagging or insulting the reader. Carefully worked-out arguments – clearly expressed and with separate points that are logically ordered – can be very effective. • *Explanation* must be clearly focused on exactly what it is that the reader needs to understand. Always look for evidence that the child understands what he or she is trying to explain. You cannot provide a clear explanation of something that you do not understand.	Paper 13c) Paper 14b) Paper 15c)	Paper 17c)
Discussion • As above, look for clarity of thinking and expression, as well as evidence that the child has some understanding of the issue under discussion. • Strong opinions are not needed: being able to see several sides to a question is a valuable skill. • Simple sentences may work best in writing of this kind.	Paper 14c) Paper 15c)	Paper 16b) Paper 17c) Paper 18b
Conversation and dialogue • Some questions invite the child to write a conversation, develop or create one or more characters, or speak in the voice of a particular character. Since we do not all speak in the same way, written conversation should convey a sense of the speaker, the context and the subject matter. • All conversation should be correctly set out and punctuated.	Paper 13b) Paper 15b)	Paper 16a) Paper 17b)

Paper 13
English skills

1–5	"Help!" cried the injured climber faintly. "I'm over here. Can't you see me?" *An exclamation mark could be used after 'here', to replace the full stop.*
6	typifies
7	salivate
8	halve
9	identify
10	nauseates
11	tears/tiers
12	plain/plane
13	pear/pair
14	pours/pores
15	leak/leek
16	variety
17	flight
18	servitude
19	compositions
20	deception
21	assist
22	agile
23	learned
24	nurtured
25	sleuth

There are several possible answers to questions 26–30. Those given are examples only.

26	rather slapdash and makeshift, not perfectly done
27	neat, clean and tidy
28	family, friends and neighbours
29	everyone
30	invalid, without value, of no legal or other worth
31	aqueduct
32	century
33	navy
34	octopus *or* octopod
35	decimate (This word is now used to mean *to greatly reduce numbers*.)

Paper 13 – *continued*

36	phantom
37	blazing inferno
38	salamander
39	cider
40	murder
41	logical
42	informative
43	delirious
44	despotic
45	loathsome
46	loquacious
47	eloquent
48	veracity
49	reticent
50	voracity
51	sign
52	tick
53	lap
54	bay
55	sum
56	quadrilateral
57	quadruped
58	quadruple
59	quadruplets
60	quadrant

Comprehension

61	C
62	A
63	A
64	B
65	D
66	D
67	A
68	C
69	A
70	C
71	B
72	D practise (*should be 'practice'*)
73	C compleet (*should be 'complete'*)
74	C mesure (*should be 'measure'*)
75	A wieght (*should be 'weight'*)

Paper 13 – *continued*

Short writing task

Refer to general guidelines on page A4 and specific notes on page A5 as indicated.

a)	Story writing
b)	Concise description, Conversation and dialogue
c)	Instructions, persuasive writing and explanations

Paper 14
English skills

1–5	"That was an interesting story," said Mrs Patel, smiling. "Could you put in some pictures now?" "But I'm rubbish at drawing," replied Henry.
6	carelessness
7	dilemma
8	arsonist
9	round
10	senseless
11	condense
12	antihistamine
13	supernatural
14	profusion
15	disapproving
16	festivity, festivities, feasting
17	contravention
18	continuity
19	convalescence
20	dramatist
21	"I haven't heard the post arrive this morning," *or* "I didn't hear the post arrive this morning," remarked Shabana.
22	"How much are the cakes, please?" *or* "What is the price of the cakes, please?" Louis asked the shop assistant.
23	"Stand up, everyone," *or* "Everyone/everybody stand up," said the teacher.
24	"Come and help!" the mechanic shouted to his apprentice.
25	"[I'm afraid] a severe storm is on its way," warned the Captain.
26	enigmatic
27	neurotic
28	clear
29	rhythmic *or* rhythmical
30	dogmatic

Paper 14 – *continued*

31	contradict
32	contraflow
33	controversial
34	contrary
35	contraband
36	eyes and eye diseases
37	animals
38	the heart and heart conditions
39	nerves and diseases of the nervous system
40	the mind and behaviour
41	lying
42	lain
43	laid *or* lays
44	laid
45	laid
46	Please could we have lasagne for dinner? *or* Could we have lasagne for dinner please?
47	Our holiday in Disneyland was a bit of a disaster.
48	Animals who hibernate must have very long dreams.
49	Because of the strike, the rehearsal started late. *or* The rehearsal started late because of the strike.
50	I would be slimmer if chocolate were less delicious. *or* If chocolate were less delicious I would be slimmer.
51	complement
52	implement
53	implement
54	competent
55	compliment
56	knowledge
57	aerial
58	accommodation
59	biscuit
60	business

Paper 14 – *continued*
Comprehension

61	B
62	D
63	B
64	D
65	B
66	C
67	A
68	B
69	C
70	C
71	C
72	B
73	B
74	B
75	C

Short writing task

Refer to general guidelines on page A4 and specific notes on page A5 as indicated.

a)	Story writing, Concise description
b)	Instructions, persuasive writing and explanations
c)	Discussion

Paper 15
English skills

1–5 | Venita, a brilliant tennis player, won her match – though, sadly, she fell, straining her wrist and breaking her mum's racquet.
A comma could be used after 'match', if preferred. Then dashes could replace the commas before and after 'sadly'.

6 | infuriates
7 | portend
8 | bathed
9 | encircled *or* circled
10 | accompany

11 | She didn't speak very clearly.
12 | The teacher taught him many facts. *or* The teacher learned many facts.
13 | My friend and I went shopping.
14 | He was so helpful [that] I could have hugged him.
15 | My brother laid the table for tea.

16 | beautiful *or* beautious, beautifully, beautify
17 | secret *or* secretive, secretly *or* secretively, secrete
18 | weak, weakly, weaken
19 | dark, darkly, darken
20 | glorious, gloriously, glorify

21 | It would be very exciting to find buried treasure.
22 | Joe's parents have adopted a little girl called Alice.
23 | Poppies grow all over the battlefields of northern France. *or* Poppies grow all over the northern battlefields of France.
The words 'all over' may also be reversed to read 'over all'.

Paper 15 – *continued*

24 | I think Lego is the best toy ever invented.
25 | I love dogs but my friend prefers cats. *or* I love cats but my friend prefers dogs.

26 | vegetarian
27 | botany
28 | amphibious
29 | inflammable
30 | antidote

31 | lane
32 | maxim
33 | chisel
34 | robust
35 | second

36 | octagon
37 | octet
38 | October
39 | octocentenary
40 | octave

41 | remedy
42 | delay
43 | aggressive
44 | first
45 | killer

46 | percussion
47 | woodwind
48 | strings
49 | brass
50 | keyboards

51 | perspiration
52 | fragrance
53 | drowsiness
54 | alertness
55 | harassment

56 | effect
57 | effect
58 | affected
59 | affect
60 | effective

Paper 15 – *continued*
Comprehension

61 | C
62 | C
63 | A
64 | C
65 | C
66 | A
67 | D
68 | B
69 | A
70 | B
71 | A
72 | C
73 | D
74 | B
75 | A

Short writing task

Refer to general guidelines on page A4 and specific notes on page A5 as indicated.

a) | Story writing, Concise description
b) | Conversation and dialogue
c) | Instructions, persuasive writing and explanations, Discussion

Paper 16
English skills

1–5 | "Gently does it," said the farmer as the new lamb plopped onto the straw, shook itself and tried to stand.
A comma could be used after the word 'itself', if desired.

6 | superfluous *should be* superstitious
7 | obliterate *should be* illiterate
8 | ineligible *should be* illegible
9 | histrionics *should be* hysterics
10 | affluence *should be* influence

11 | recluse
12 | scruffy
13 | efface
14 | poisonous
15 | burdensome

16 | conscionce *should be* conscience
17 | exibition *should be* exhibition
18 | surgen *should be* surgeon
19 | soliciter *should be* solicitor
20 | playwrite *should be* playwright

21 | laughed, giggled, ran
22 | bit
23 | arrived
24 | said, was, watch
25 | come, shouted, ran

26 | cemetery
27 | mediocre
28 | spontaneous
29 | lackadaisical
30 | vague

31 | The trouble with computer games is that it's really hard to stop.

Paper 16 – *continued*

32 | Snails carry their homes with them wherever they go. *or* Wherever they go, snails carry their homes with them.
33 | I have relations all over the world. *or* I have relations all the world over.
34 | My favourite meal is pizza with olives and mushrooms. *or* My favourite meal is pizza with mushrooms and olives. *or* Pizza with olives and mushrooms is my favourite meal.
35 | It rained all day on my birthday. *or* On my birthday it rained all day.

36 | crosses
37 | formulae *or* formulas
38 | phenomena
39 | thieves
40 | fathers-in-law

41 | mournful
42 | decisive
43 | global
44 | talkative
45 | nervous *or* nervy

46 | has a silver lining
47 | is next to godliness
48 | before they're hatched *or* before they hatch *or* before they've hatched
49 | be bygones
50 | choosers

51 | leisure
52 | grammar
53 | maintenance
54 | description
55 | memorise

56 | paced
57 | palate
58 | paste
59 | pallet
60 | palette

Paper 16 – *continued*
Comprehension

61 | C
62 | A
63 | D
64 | B
65 | C
66 | B
67 | A
68 | B
69 | A
70 | C
71 | C
72 | C affects (*should be* 'effects')
73 | B concreet (*should be* 'concrete')
74 | B idear (*should be* 'idea')
75 | B wellfare (*should be* 'welfare')

Short writing task

Refer to general guidelines on page A4 and specific notes on page A5 as indicated.

a) | Story writing, Conversation and dialogue
b) | Discussion
c) | Detailed description

Paper 17
English skills

1–5 | "Vivie, have you got the picnic?" called Lucas. "'Cos I need to put in the tomatoes and Dad's cheesy things." "He didn't want the cheesy things," replied Vivie, "so I ate them."
An exclamation mark could be used to replace the second and/or third full stop (after 'things' and 'them').

6 | clockwork
7 | ditchwater
8 | bone
9 | pikestaff
10 | hatter

11 | repetition *or* repeat, repetitious *or* repetitive *or* repeated, repetitively *or* repeatedly, (repeat)
12 | vileness *or* vilification, (vile), vilely, vilify
13 | derisiveness *or* derider *or* derision, derisive *or* derisible *or* derisory, derisively *or* deridingly, (deride)
14 | simplicity *or* simpleton *or* simplification, (simple), simply, simplify
15 | (nation), national, nationally, nationalise

16 | sink
17 | fathom
18 | second
19 | lead
20 | obtuse

Paper 17 – *continued*

21 | synagogue
22 | dialogue
23 | prologue
24 | monologue
25 | epilogue
You might point out to the child that the 'a' should be changed to 'an' as this last word begins with a vowel, but still give a mark if this change has not been made.

26 | orderly
27 | opaque
28 | lustrous
29 | emphatic
30 | sullen

31 | container
32 | liquid
33 | ingredient
34 | dwelling
35 | metal

36 | ingenuous *should be* ingenious
37 | magnet *should be* magnate
38 | personal *should be* personnel *or* persons *or* people
39 | mute *should be* moot
40 | peak *should be* pique

41 | motorbike
42 | pliers
43 | Spoonerism
44 | Sheep
45 | river

46 | gruesome
47 | acquiesce
48 | juvenile
49 | destroy
50 | trim

51 | disembark
52 | irregular
53 | unimaginative
54 | inappropriate
55 | discourtesy

Paper 17 – *continued*

56 | in *or* by *or* with
57 | to
58 | with
59 | at
60 | out

Comprehension

61 | C
62 | C
63 | B
64 | B
65 | B
66 | C
67 | C
68 | A
69 | B
70 | C
71 | A
72 | B
73 | A
74 | D
75 | C

Short writing task

Refer to general guidelines on page A4 and specific notes on page A5 as indicated.

a) | Story writing, Detailed description
b) | Conversation and dialogue
c) | Concise description, Instructions, persuasive writing and explanations, Discussion

Paper 18
English skills

1–5 | "There's no point in going now."
"Why not?"
"Because we've missed the bus."
"But can't we walk there?"
"Are you crazy?"

6 | between
7 | amongst *or* among
8 | to
9 | by *or* at
10 | around *or* round

11 | fossil
12 | meteor
13 | spinach
14 | sultan
15 | parole

16 | mathematics
17 | mechanic
18 | florist
19 | archaeologist
20 | imaginary

21 | to hit below the belt
22 | to flog a dead horse
23 | as the crow flies
24 | like a bull in a china shop
25 | to bury the hatchet

26 | fame
27 | reject
28 | relish
29 | pierce
30 | slanting

31 | She (P) pushed (V) vigorously (ADV).
32 | They (P) came (V) here (ADV).
33 | We (P) met (V) before (ADV).
34 | There (ADV) it (P) was (V).
35 | She (P) ran (V) limply (ADV) then (ADV) suddenly (ADV) fell (V).

Paper 18 – *continued*

36 | He and I were playing in the park.
37 | The car passed me at great speed.
38 | He has led me up the garden path.
39 | Can I borrow your pen for a while?
40 | She lent me five pounds for my lunch.

41 | wakeful
42 | demented
43 | duvet
44 | dream
45 | late

46 | geometric *or* geometrical
47 | intellectual
48 | partial
49 | daily
50 | elusive

51 | reserve
52 | triplets
53 | requested
54 | formerly
55 | course

56 | content<u>ment</u>
57 | neighbour<u>hood</u>
58 | mechan<u>ism</u>
59 | in<u>edible</u>
60 | psych<u>ology</u>

Comprehension

61 | B
62 | B
63 | A
64 | C
65 | B
66 | D
67 | C
68 | A
69 | B
70 | B
71 | C
72 | A
73 | C
74 | B
75 | C

Paper 18 – *continued*

Short writing task

Refer to general guidelines on page A4 and specific notes on page A5 as indicated.

a) | Story writing, Detailed description
b) | Discussion
c) | Detailed description

This book of answers is a pull-out section from
English Progress Papers 3

Published by **Schofield & Sims Ltd**
Dogley Mill, Fenay Bridge, Huddersfield HD8 0NQ, UK
Telephone 01484 607080
www.schofieldandsims.co.uk

First published in 1993
This edition copyright © Schofield & Sims Ltd, 2018

Authors: **Patrick Berry and Susan Hamlyn**
Patrick Berry and Susan Hamlyn have asserted their moral rights
under the Copyright, Designs and Patents Act, 1988, to be identified
as the authors of this work.

British Library Cataloguing in Publication Data
A catalogue record for this book is available from the British Library.

Design by **Ledgard Jepson Ltd**

Printed in the UK by **Page Bros (Norwich) Ltd**

ISBN 978 07217 1475 2

Q. 76–85 Short writing task

MARK

Write for 20–30 minutes on *one* of the following. Continue on a separate sheet if you need to.

a) The Surprise

b) You are Amber, home at last after the tour referred to in 'The Day that Changed my Summer' (page 24). Write the conversation you have with your best friend on the first occasion you meet after your return.

c) Some people think music is an important school subject while others disagree. Your headteacher is deciding whether or not to include music lessons for everyone in the timetable and has invited pupils to write giving their opinions. Write giving your views.

27

SHORT WRITING TASK SUB-TOTAL	10
English skills sub-total (from page 23)	60
Comprehension sub-total (from page 26)	30
Short writing task sub-total (from this page)	10
PAPER 15 TOTAL MARK	100

START HERE

Q. 1–60 English skills

MARK

Q. 1–5 punctuation	Rewrite the sentence correctly, adding the necessary punctuation.

gently does it said the farmer as the new lamb plopped onto the straw shook itself and tried to stand

_____

_____

_____

1–5 [ ] 5

Q. 6–10 word choice	Find the word that is used wrongly. Underline it. Then write the correct word on the line.

6 He is superfluous and won't walk under ladders. _____   6 [ ] 1

7 She can't read or write and is obliterate. _____   7 [ ] 1

8 I could not read his ineligible writing. _____   8 [ ] 1

9 Meg had histrionics when she saw the spider. _____   9 [ ] 1

10 No-one drives well under the affluence of alcohol. _____   10 [ ] 1

Q. 11–15 word meanings, synonyms	Underline the *one* word that is closest in meaning to the word shown in capitals.

11 HERMIT   frog, wizard, recluse, alone   11 [ ] 1

12 UNKEMPT   empty, free, scruffy, independent   12 [ ] 1

13 ERASE   efface, hope, lower, lift   13 [ ] 1

14 TOXIC   daft, poisonous, spotty, ticking   14 [ ] 1

15 ONEROUS   twice, numerous, burdensome, tired   15 [ ] 1

MARK [   ]

English skills

MARK

Q. 16–20 spelling	Find the word that is spelt wrongly. Underline it. Then write it correctly on the line.

16 I have a bad conscionce about the broken window.   _____   16 1

17 We went to a brilliant astronomy exibition at the museum. _____   17 1

18 I'd like to be a hospital surgen when I grow up.   _____   18 1

19 A soliciter helps when you have a legal problem.   _____   19 1

20 Shakespeare is the world's most famous playwrite.   _____   20 1

Q. 21–25 verbs	Underline the verb(s).

21 They laughed and giggled as they ran home.   21 1

22 The angry gardener bit the dog.   22 1

23 I arrived 20 minutes late for the appointment.   23 1

24 Mansoor said he was going to watch the match.   24 1

25 "Come here!" she shouted as Daniel ran away.   25 1

Q. 26–30 spelling	Read the clue. Fill in the missing letters to make the word.

26 a burial ground   c _ _ _ _ _ _ _   26 1

27 of average quality, not special   m _ _ _ _ c _ _ _   27 1

28 involuntary or unthinking   s p _ _ _ _ _ e _ _ s   28 1

29 sloppy, couldn't care less   l _ _ k _ d _ _ _ _ c _ _   29 1

30 mentally uncertain or vacant   v _ _ u _   30 1

MARK

English skills

MARK

Q. 31–35	Unscramble the sentence so that it makes sense. Write the sentence on the line. Include capital letters and punctuation as needed.	

unscramble
sentences

31 hard trouble stop computer is the that really it's with to games

_____

_____   31   1

32 go carry with homes snails them they their wherever

_____   32   1

33 relations i all world the have over

_____   33   1

34 with my meal is olives mushrooms pizza and favourite

_____

_____   34   1

35 rained day birthday all on it my

_____   35   1

Q. 36–40

plurals

Write the plural.

36 cross   _____   36   1

37 formula   _____   37   1

38 phenomenon   _____   38   1

39 thief   _____   39   1

40 father-in-law   _____   40   1

Q. 41–45

adjectives

Add to the sentence an adjective that is made from the word shown in capitals.

41 MOURN   The choir sang a _____ song.   41   1

42 DECIDE   We won a _____ victory in the match.   42   1

43 GLOBE   Scientists warn us that _____ warming is dangerous.   43   1

44 TALK   The _____ class was asked to be quiet.   44   1

45 NERVE   I felt very _____ walking through the forest.   45   1

MARK [   ]

English skills

MARK

Q. 46–50	Complete the proverb or saying.		

proverbs and sayings

46 Every cloud _____ . 　　46 　1

47 Cleanliness _____ . 　　47 　1

48 Don't count your chickens _____ . 　　48 　1

49 Let bygones _____ . 　　49 　1

50 Beggars can't be _____ . 　　50 　1

Q. 51–55	Read the clue. Fill in the missing letters to make the word.

spelling

51 time to enjoy yourself 　　　　　　　l _ _ _ _ _ _ 　　51 　1

52 the rules of language 　　　　　　　g _ _ _ _ _ _ 　　52 　1

53 keeping something in working order 　　m _ _ _ _ _ _ _ _ c e 　　53 　1

54 an account of what something is like 　　d _ _ _ _ _ _ _ _ _ _ 　　54 　1

55 to learn something by heart 　　　　m _ _ _ _ _ _ _ 　　55 　1

Q. 56–60	Put the word in the sentence where it makes the best sense.

word choice　　　palate, palette, pallet, paced, paste

56 The student _____ up and down awaiting her exam results. 　　56 　1

57 It is said that expensive wines please the _____. 　　57 　1

58 I'll cut and _____ the pictures onto my webpage. 　　58 　1

59 The safe waited on a _____ for collection. 　　59 　1

60 The artist mixed his colours on a _____. 　　60 　1

MARK 　☐

ENGLISH SKILLS SUB-TOTAL 　☐ 　60

MARK

Read this passage carefully.

Recycling in Victorian Times

Some see recycling as a concept that is relatively new. However, the 'dustmen' of the nineteenth and early twentieth centuries played a vital role in the recycling of ash.

It's something we've always done. Societies going back to ancient times have collected their waste materials and processed them to be used again, often as something else. In Victorian Britain,
5 the most prolific recyclers were the 'dustmen'. These were not the essential rubbish-collectors of today but men who drove carts round their local neighbourhood and collected the ash – the 'dust' – from the fires that everyone used to heat their homes
10 and cook their meals. In the days before homes were heated and lit by electricity and gas you can imagine how much dust there was to collect.

The dustmen particularly liked wet days when the ashes were damp and clouds of dust would
15 not choke them. The dust was very bad for them, getting into their throats and lungs. The men were also notorious for their drinking, demanding a mug of beer for every load they collected, to clear their throats. What with the damaging dust and the
20 constant beer, few dustmen grew old.

The dustmen worked as close as possible to canals or rivers. London dustmen would load their great heaps of dust onto barges, which would carry the billowing mountains down to the brickworks in
25 Kent. The ash was decanted onto even bigger mountains where old men and women (there were no pensions in those days) worked as sifters – separating the fine dust that would be turned into new bricks from the rubbish and grit. The dust
30 was mixed with clay, formed into bricks and baked in kilns. The baked bricks were then loaded into carts and taken back up the river to build, perhaps, more fireplaces or ovens to burn more coal and wood into ashes.

35 Today far fewer people in Britain heat their homes or cook using coal or wood, but coal is still a huge industry and scientists have identified innovative ways of isolating some of the valuable metal ores and minerals in coal ash. On a planet with an ever-
40 growing population and finite natural resources, this presents an exciting opportunity to look at ash from a very different point of view from that of the Victorian dustmen and to recycle it in ways they couldn't have imagined.

Now read these questions. You have a choice of four answers to each question. Choose the *one* answer you think the best. Draw a line in the box next to its letter, like this.

A ▭

61 Which of the following points is made in the first two sentences?

A There have always been clubs for rubbish collecting.
B Rubbish is usually very old.
C Recycling is nothing new.
D People have always collected rubbish.

61 · 2

62 Line 5 tells us that the most prolific recyclers were the 'dustmen'. What does this tell us about the dustmen?

A that they were the people who did the most recycling
B that they were the dirtiest recyclers
C that they were the most energetic recyclers
D that they were the people who recycled most cheaply

62 · 2

MARK ▭

Comprehension

MARK

63 What was the 'dust' that they collected?

A the ash from candles   A ☐
B the ash floating about in the atmosphere   B ☐
C burnt rubbish   C ☐
D the ash from coal and wood fires   D ☐   63   2

64 Which sort of weather do you imagine the dustmen disliked the most?

A heatwaves   A ☐
B windy days   B ☐
C snow   C ☐
D hailstones   D ☐   64   2

65 We are told in line 20 that 'few dustmen grew old'. Which of the following is *not* a reason for this?

A repeated choking   A ☐
B alcohol poisoning   B ☐
C working in the rain   C ☐
D damaged lungs   D ☐   65   2

66 Lines 21–22 say that 'The dustmen worked as close as possible to canals or rivers'. Why was this the case?

A because it was healthier   A ☐
B because canals and rivers provided transport systems   B ☐
C because the dustmen owned the barges   C ☐
D because there were lots of canals and rivers in Kent   D ☐   66   2

67 Which of the following would a 'sifter' (line 27) have used?

A a sieve   A ☐
B a sifting machine   B ☐
C a seive   C ☐
D a separator   D ☐   67   2

68 What is a 'kiln' (line 31)?

A a factory   A ☐
B an oven   B ☐
C a batch of 20   C ☐
D 10 kilograms in weight   D ☐   68   2

MARK

Comprehension

MARK

69 What is the point made in lines 31–34?

    A The ashes collected by the dustmen are part of a cycle.

    B The bricks have been made from ashes.

    C People are using too much coal and wood.

    D The river is useful for moving ash and bricks.

A ☐ B ☐ C ☐ D ☐   69   2

70 'Innovative' (line 37) means 'new'. Which of the following words means 'a new arrangement or change'?

    A notation

    B novel

    C innovation

    D notion

A ☐ B ☐ C ☐ D ☐   70   2

71 The first sentence in the final paragraph tells us all but one of the following. Identify the piece of information that it does *not* provide.

    A Coal is still an important aspect of commercial life.

    B Scientists can separate precious elements from coal ash.

    C No-one any longer needs the dust and ash from coal.

    D There are now few domestic users of coal.

A ☐ B ☐ C ☐ D ☐   71   2

Find the spelling mistake. Underline it and write the box letter at the end of the line.

72 Constant toil with   harmful ash had   disastrous affects on   dustmen's respiration.

    A   B   C   D   ☐   72   2

73 Many people believe   that concreet   is less attractive than   traditional bricks.

    A   B   C   D   ☐   73   2

74 It is a distressing   idear that senior   citizens were forced   to work till death.

    A   B   C   D   ☐   74   2

75 Today we have   the wellfare state   to provide pensions   and care from taxes.

    A   B   C   D   ☐   75   2

MARK ☐

COMPREHENSION SUB-TOTAL ☐ 30

Q. 76–85 Short writing task

MARK

Write for 20–30 minutes on *one* of the following. Continue on a separate sheet if you need to.

a) Write a story that begins like this.

> "Why not? What are you on about?" She looked bored.
> "That's plastic! And those are glass. You have to recycle them."
> "I really can't be bothered."

b) If I were a scientist I would . . .

c) When people used to burn coal and wood every day, cities used to fill up with fog. These fogs were called 'pea-soupers' because they were so dense. Imagine taking a walk around your local area on a day when it is impossible to see more than a metre ahead. Describe the experience.

_____

_____

_____

_____

_____

_____

_____

_____

_____

_____

_____

_____

_____

_____

_____

_____

_____

_____

_____

_____

ND OF TEST

SHORT WRITING TASK SUB-TOTAL	10
English skills sub-total (from page 31)	60
Comprehension sub-total (from page 34)	30
Short writing task sub-total (from this page)	10
PAPER 16 TOTAL MARK	100

Paper 17

Q. 1–60 English skills

MARK

Q. 1–5

punctuation

Rewrite the text correctly, adding the necessary punctuation.

vivie have you got the picnic called lucas cos i need to put in the tomatoes and dads cheesy things he didn't want the cheesy things replied vivie so i ate them

_____

_____

_____

_____

| 1–5 | 5 |

Q. 6–10

similes

Put the word in the simile to which it belongs.

pikestaff, clockwork, bone, ditchwater, hatter

6 as regular as   _____ | 6 | 1 |

7 as dull as   _____ | 7 | 1 |

8 as dry as a   _____ | 8 | 1 |

9 as plain as a   _____ | 9 | 1 |

10 as mad as a   _____ | 10 | 1 |

Q. 11–15

parts of speech, nouns, adjectives, adverbs, verbs

Write the missing parts of speech of the word shown in capitals.

	NOUN	ADJECTIVE	ADVERB	VERB	
Example:	ICE	_icy_	_icily_	_ice_	
11	_____	_____	_____	REPEAT	11 1
12	_____	VILE	_____		12 1
13	_____	_____	_____	DERIDE	13 1
14	_____	SIMPLE	_____	_____	14 1
15	NATION	_____		_____	15 1

MARK

English skills   MARK

Q. 16–20 homonyms	Write the *one* word that has *both* meanings.		
	16 to lower or drop, especially in water / the place for washing up _____	16	1
	17 to work out the answer to a problem / six feet, measured under water _____	17	1
	18 supporter in a duel or fight / a tiny length of time _____	18	1
	19 to go in front / attached to a dog's collar for walks _____	19	1
	20 greater than a right angle / dull witted _____	20	1

Q. 21–25 word choice	Put the word in the sentence where it makes the best sense.		
	prologue, monologue, dialogue, epilogue, synagogue		
	21 A _____ is a place of worship for Jewish people.	21	1
	22 A _____ is a conversation between two or more people.	22	1
	23 A _____ is an introduction to a poem or a play.	23	1
	24 A _____ is a speech for just one person.	24	1
	25 A _____ is the end part of a book or play.	25	1

Q. 26–30 adjectives	Add to the sentence an adjective that is made from the word shown in capitals.		
	26 ORDER They left the hall in an _____ fashion.	26	1
	27 OPACITY The glass is _____ and I can't see through it.	27	1
	28 LUSTRE The _____ diamond gleamed in the moonlight.	28	1
	29 EMPHASIS The crowd encouraged me with an _____ cheer.	29	1
	30 SULLENNESS The _____ and private man had few friends.	30	1

MARK [   ]

English skills

MARK

Q. 31–35	Underline the *one* word that may be used to describe all the others.	
word groups (by meaning)	**31** box, container, sack, holdall, crate	31 1
	32 paraffin, water, liquid, petrol, lemonade	32 1
	33 ingredient, flour, water, raisins, butter	33 1
	34 dwelling, house, bungalow, flat, maisonette	34 1
	35 copper, lead, iron, zinc, metal	35 1

Q. 36–40	Find the word that is used wrongly. Underline it. Then write the correct word on the line.	
word choice	**36** I have an ingenuous scheme for making money. _____	36 1
	37 He is a famous business magnet. _____	37 1
	38 "How many personal work here?" he asked. _____	38 1
	39 "It's a mute point, I'm afraid, and we may not agree." _____	39 1
	40 In a fit of peak she left the room. _____	40 1

Q. 41–45	Underline the *one* word that is the odd one out.	
odd one out (by meaning)	**41** canoe, glider, motorbike, parachute, bicycle	41 1
	42 lancet, pliers, scalpel, forceps, stethoscope	42 1
	43 Islam, Judaism, Christianity, Spoonerism, Buddhism	43 1
	44 Goat, Twins, Ram, Scorpion, Sheep	44 1
	45 ocean, lake, sea, river, pool	45 1

MARK

English skills   MARK

Q. 46–50

word meanings, synonyms

Underline the *one* word that is closest in meaning to the word shown in capitals.

46 MACABRE   shaded, odd, gruesome, raincoat   46   1

47 RELENT   acquiesce, borrow, fasten, connive   47   1

48 IMMATURE   heavy, dangerous, jocose, juvenile   48   1

49 ANNIHILATE   desiccate, destroy, contemplate, delicate   49   1

50 PRUNE   custard, trim, twerp, desert   50   1

Q. 51–55

antonyms, prefixes

Write down the antonym (opposite) of the word, using a prefix.

51 embark   _____   51   1

52 regular   _____   52   1

53 imaginative   _____   53   1

54 appropriate   _____   54   1

55 courtesy   _____   55   1

Q. 56–60

prepositions

Add the preposition that best completes the sentence.

56 I was disappointed _____ the performance.   56   1

57 We are closed _____ visitors.   57   1

58 Can you put up _____ sausages yet again?   58   1

59 He expressed surprise _____ the arrival of my mum.   59   1

60 I hurt my thumb and had to sit _____ the rest of the match.   60   1

MARK

ENGLISH SKILLS SUB-TOTAL   60

Q. 61–75 Comprehension   MARK

Read this passage carefully.

Sheep Shearing

Shearing sheep for their wool has been important to farmers for many thousands of years.
This description of the sheep-shearing process was first published in 1912.

From early morning there had been bleating
of sheep in the yard, so that one knew the creatures
were being sheared, and toward evening I went
along to see. Thirty or forty naked-looking ghosts
5 of sheep were penned against the barn and perhaps
a dozen still inhabiting their coats.

Into the wool of one of these bulky ewes the
farmer's small, yellow-haired daughter was twisting
her fist, hustling it toward Fate. Though pulled
10 almost off her feet by the frightened, stubborn
creature, she never let go, till, with a despairing
cough, the ewe had passed over the threshold and
was fast in the hands of a shearer. At the far end
of the barn, close by the doors, I stood a minute
15 or two before shifting up to watch the shearing.
Into that dim, beautiful home of age, with its
great rafters and mellow stone archways, the June
sunlight shone through loopholes and chinks,
in thin glamour, powdering with its very
20 strangeness the dark cathedraled air, where, high
up, clung a fog of old grey cobwebs so thick as ever
were the stalactites of a huge cave. At this end the
scent of sheep and wool and men had not yet routed

that home essence of the barn, like the savour
25 of acorns and withering beech leaves.

Sitting on the creatures, or with a leg firmly crooked
over their heads, each shearer, even the two boys,
had an air of going at it in his own way. In their
white canvas shearing suits they worked very
30 steadily, almost in silence, as if drowsed by the
'click-clip, click-clip' of the shears. And the sheep,
but for an occasional wriggle of legs or head, lay
quiet enough, having an inborn sense perhaps of the
fitness of things, even when, once in a way, they lost
35 more than wool. They were glad too, mayhap,
to be rid of their matted vestments. And always
there was the buzz of flies swarming in the sunlight
of the open doorway, the dry rustle of the pollarded
lime-trees in the sharp wind outside, the bleating
40 of some released ewe, upset at her own nakedness,
the scrape and shuffle of heels and sheep's limbs
on the floor, together with the 'click-clip, click-clip'
of the shears.

Abridged and adapted from *Sheep Shearing* by John
Galsworthy (1867–1933)

Now read these questions. You have a choice of four answers
to each question. Choose the *one* answer you think the best.
Draw a line in the box next to its letter, like this.

A ▭

61 Which of the following is another word for the wool that covers a sheep?

    A hide

    B pelt

    C fleece

    D fur

                                                            61   2

62 Why do lines 4–5 refer to the 'naked-looking ghosts of sheep'?

    A because the sheep are not really there

    B because the sheep are now dead

    C because the sheep look eerie and insubstantial without their coats

    D because the sheep are white and thin

                                                            62   2

MARK ▭

Comprehension

63 How many sheep have yet to be sheared?

- A about forty
- B about twelve
- C several
- D about thirty

63   2

64 What was the farmer's daughter doing?

- A hurting the sheep
- B pushing the sheep towards the shearer
- C bullying the sheep
- D stroking the sheep

64   2

65 Which word in the second paragraph means the same as 'obstinate'?

- A bulky
- B stubborn
- C despairing
- D ewe

65   2

66 What is a barn?

- A the wall of a farmhouse
- B a closed-off area for keeping sheep in
- C a farm building in which animals or crops are housed
- D a farmyard in which animals are fed

66   2

67 Which word best completes the sentence below?

The sheep look far thinner once they are _____.

- A sheared
- B shaven
- C shorn
- D shored

67   2

68 In paragraph 2, the barn is described as the 'dim, beautiful home of age' (line 16). What does this make it sound like?

- A a dark and ancient place, made lovely by time
- B a warm, dark, foggy cave
- C a weird, neglected, creepy place
- D an underground place where little sunlight penetrates

68   2

69 Stalactites (line 22) are found hanging *down* from the *roof* of a cave. What might you find growing *up* from the *floor* of a cave?

- A satellites
- B stalagmites
- C smarties
- D ammonites

69   2

MARK

Comprehension

MARK

70 Which of the following words or phrases does *not* apply to the manner and behaviour of the shearers?

    A as if hypnotised

    B efficient

    C clumsy

    D independent

A ☐
B ☐
C ☐
D ☐   **70**   2

71 Which of the following, based on the final paragraph, is John Galsworthy *not* telling us?

    A that the sheep fought back against the shearer

    B that the sheep quite liked losing their coats

    C that the sheep's skin was sometimes cut by the shearer

    D that the sheep seemed to find the shearing appropriate

A ☐
B ☐
C ☐
D ☐   **71**   2

72 What is a male sheep called?

    A a ewe

    B a ram

    C a bull

    D a stallion

A ☐
B ☐
C ☐
D ☐   **72**   2

73 How would you describe the atmosphere of the passage – despite the hard work of the shearers?

    A peaceful

    B sad

    C noisy

    D smelly

A ☐
B ☐
C ☐
D ☐   **73**   2

74 Which word best completes the sentence below?

    Sheep shearing is _____ work.

    A seasoning

    B seasoned

    C seasonable

    D seasonal

A ☐
B ☐
C ☐
D ☐   **74**   2

75 The writer, John Galsworthy, looks closely at things. Which of the following words might best be used to describe him?

    A impressionable

    B inspective

    C observant

    D spectacular

A ☐
B ☐
C ☐
D ☐   **75**   2

MARK ☐

COMPREHENSION SUB-TOTAL ☐   3

Q. 76–85 Short writing task

MARK

Write for 20–30 minutes on *one* of the following. Continue on a separate sheet if you need to.

a) A Very Old Building

b) You are a sheep and have just had your first experience of shearing. Write the conversation you have with your friend who is awaiting his or her turn.

c) Many farms now welcome visitors, especially from schools. Do you think children from towns ought to visit farms to see what they produce and how? Write an article for your school magazine in which you discuss this question.

ND OF TEST

SHORT WRITING TASK SUB-TOTAL		10
English skills sub-total (from page 39)		60
Comprehension sub-total (from page 42)		30
Short writing task sub-total (from this page)		10
PAPER 17 TOTAL MARK		100

Paper 18

START HERE

Q. 1–60 English skills   MARK

Q. 1–5 punctuation	Rewrite the dialogue correctly, adding the necessary punctuation. theres no point in going now why not because weve missed the bus but cant we walk there are you crazy _____ _____ _____ _____ _____

1–5   5

Q. 6–10 prepositions	Complete the sentence by adding the correct preposition. 6 Divide the sweets _____ the twins. 7 Divide these sweets _____ the four of you. 8 I object _____ your attitude. 9 He was dismayed _____ the news. 10 We worked _____ the clock to finish on time.

6   1

7   1

8   1

9   1

10   1

Q. 11–15 anagrams	Unscramble the anagram to fit the meaning given. 11 LOSSIF (found in rock) _____ 12 TOMEER (flies through the sky) _____ 13 PCHAINS (a green vegetable) _____ 14 UNLAST (Muslim ruler) _____ 15 OR LEAP (temporary release from prison) _____

11   1

12   1

13   1

14   1

15   1

MARK

English skills   MARK

Q. 16–20

spelling, word meanings

Read the clue. Fill in the missing letters to make the word.

16 the science of numbers   m _ _ _ _ _ _ _ _ _   16   1

17 a mender of cars   m _ _ _ _ _ _ _   17   1

18 a seller of flowers   f _ _ _ _ _ _ _   18   1

19 a person who digs for relics   a _ _ _ _ _ _ _ _ _ _ _ _   19   1

20 existing only in your mind   i _ _ _ _ _ _ _ _ _   20   1

Q. 21–25

popular phrases

Write the popular phrase next to its meaning.

like a bull in a china shop, to bury the hatchet, to hit below the belt, to flog a dead horse, as the crow flies

21 to behave unfairly _____   21   1

22 to waste time or resources _____   22   1

23 in a straight line _____   23   1

24 really clumsy _____   24   1

25 to make peace _____   25   1

Q. 26–30

word meanings, synonyms

Underline the word in each line that is closest in meaning to the word shown in capitals.

26 CELEBRITY   famous, fame, famished, familiar, notorious   26   1

27 SPURN   goad, shout, jeer, reject, throw   27   1

28 SAVOUR   relish, collect, hope, disguise, welcome   28   1

29 PENETRATE   bury, scare, pierce, commit, push   29   1

30 OBLIQUE   upright, level, vertical, slanting, down   30   1

MARK

English skills

MARK

Q. 31–35 parts of speech, verbs, adverbs	Read the sentence. Write V under the verb, P under the pronoun and ADV under the adverb(s). **31** She pushed vigorously. **32** They came here. **33** We met before. **34** There it was. **35** She ran limply then suddenly fell.	**31** ☐ 1 **32** ☐ 1 **33** ☐ 1 **34** ☐ 1 **35** ☐ 1

Q. 36–40 grammar	Rewrite the sentence correctly. **36** Him and me was playing in the park. _____ **37** The car past me at great speed. _____ **38** He has lead me up the garden path. _____ **39** Can I lend your pen for a while? _____ **40** She leant me five pounds for my lunch. _____	**36** ☐ 1 **37** ☐ 1 **38** ☐ 1 **39** ☐ 1 **40** ☐ 1

Q. 41–45 odd one out (by meaning)	Underline the *one* word that is the odd one out. **41** fatigued, zonked, wakeful, tired, exhausted **42** glad, happy, demented, delighted, pleased **43** bed, cot, futon, duvet, hammock **44** sleep, slumber, dream, doze, snooze **45** final, end, late, conclusion, finish	**41** ☐ 1 **42** ☐ 1 **43** ☐ 1 **44** ☐ 1 **45** ☐ 1

MARK ☐

English skills

MARK

Q. 46–50 adjectives	Add to the sentence an adjective that is made from the word shown in capitals.		
	46 GEOMETRY We were asked to draw any _____ shape.	46	1
	47 INTELLECT The scientist's _____ ability was breathtaking.	47	1
	48 PART He gained only _____ success in the exam.	48	1
	49 DAY The _____ routine became very tedious.	49	1
	50 ELUDE I've phoned and texted him but he's very _____.	50	1

Q. 51–55 word choice	Three words appear in brackets. Underline the *one* word that completes the sentence correctly.		
	51 I'd like to (reserve, conserve, preserve) two seats for the school play.	51	1
	52 Three babies! I'm not sure I could manage (triples, triplicates, triplets).	52	1
	53 "Please bring back some pears," (requested, required, requited) Mum.	53	1
	54 "I went to that school (formally, formerly, fourmally)," said Marie.	54	1
	55 "No uniform today, of (cause, course, coarse)!" yelled Kim.	55	1

Q. 56–60 suffixes	Add the suffix that best completes the sentence.		
	hood, ology, ism, ible, ment		
	56 She purred with content_____.	56	1
	57 I want to live in a livelier neighbour_____.	57	1
	58 My brother invented a mechan_____ to make motorbikes quieter.	58	1
	59 "It's ined_____!" said Mrs Shah when she tried my apple tart.	59	1
	60 I will study psych_____ when I'm older.	60	1

MARK

ENGLISH SKILLS SUB-TOTAL   60

Q. 61–75 Comprehension

MARK

Read this passage carefully.

Before or After

I like to get there early when the cleaning
has just been finished and you can smell polish.
Or when, in the kitchen, cucumber rings and radish-
roses march all the way down the salmon and the icing
5 is perfect. Before the shop opens, when pyramids
of apples and oranges still show no sign of blemish.
When the snow is untrodden, the sheets ironed freshly
and nothing has been said that could be heard or misheard.

Or after. When scars of fires and flattened grass
10 show that the campsite has been abandoned.
When the beds are stripped and the visitors gone.
When the furniture-van drives away and the house
echoes like a cathedral. When there is no more traffic.
When everything has gone wrong that is going to go wrong
15 and they ring down the changes. And the weeds begin
to push their way up through the tarmac.

Dorothy Nimmo (1932–2001)

Now read these questions. You have a choice of four answers
to each question. Choose the *one* answer you think the best.
Draw a line in the box next to its letter, like this.

A ▭

61 Which phrase best describes the feeling of 'there' in the first line?

   A quiet and peaceful
   B fresh-smelling and clean
   C happy and relaxed
   D smart and shiny

A ▭
B ▭
C ▭
D ▭

61   2

62 Re-read the sentence starting, 'Or when, . . .' (lines 3–5). What does it describe?

   A the chopping of vegetables
   B carefully prepared party food
   C busy cooking activity
   D rings and flowers

A ▭
B ▭
C ▭
D ▭

62   2

63 The phrase 'radish-roses march all the way down the salmon' (lines 3–4) is an example of which literary technique?

   A personification
   B simile
   C military
   D metaphor

A ▭
B ▭
C ▭
D ▭

63   2

MARK ▭

Comprehension

MARK

64 The apples and oranges show 'no sign of blemish' (line 6). Why is this?

   A because they are piled in a pyramid   A ☐

   B because they come from Egypt   B ☐

   C because the shop is not yet open so no-one has touched them   C ☐

   D because the fruit is carefully piled up and perfect   D ☐   **64**   2

65 In line 8, the poet tells us 'nothing has been said that could be heard or misheard'. What does this suggest about speech?

   A that it can be kept to oneself   A ☐

   B that it can cause trouble and upset people   B ☐

   C that it can be impossible to hear   C ☐

   D that it can be said outside   D ☐   **65**   2

66 Which of the following phrases best completes the sentence?

   The first verse explains that the poet likes to arrive _____.

   A when all the work has been done   A ☐

   B when everything is still and quiet   B ☐

   C before everyone else is awake   C ☐

   D before anything has been spoiled   D ☐   **66**   2

67 What does 'scars' (line 9) refer to?

   A the injuries made by fires   A ☐

   B a frightening scene   B ☐

   C the marks left by the campers   C ☐

   D a terrible mess   D ☐   **67**   2

68 The poet says that 'the house echoes like a cathedral' (lines 12–13). Why is this the case?

   A because it is empty   A ☐

   B because it is a religious place   B ☐

   C because it is very big   C ☐

   D because it is very old   D ☐   **68**   2

69 The poet uses the word 'when' five times in the second verse. What do these 'whens' refer to?

   A a mixture of different times   A ☐

   B five different times when something is finished   B ☐

   C five quiet times   C ☐

   D five very sad times   D ☐   **69**   2

MARK

Comprehension

MARK

70 'When everything has gone wrong that is going to go wrong' – in line 14.
Which of these words is used to describe people who expect things to go wrong?

    A miserable

    B pessimistic

    C prejudiced

    D optimistic

70 2

71 What is 'tarmac' (line 16)?

    A a lawn

    B the floor of a house

    C the surface of a road

    D the pavement

71 2

72 The end of the poem refers to a time when 'the weeds begin to push their way up through the tarmac' (lines 15–16). Which of the following does this suggest?

    A that there is no-one to keep the weeds under control

    B that it is night and everyone is in bed

    C that everyone has moved away

    D that no-one cares about the weeds

72 2

73 Which of these words best describes how the speaker in the poem comes across?

    A solitaire

    B solemn

    C solitary

    D solicitous

73 2

74 The poem's title suggests that the poet prefers to avoid which of the following scenes?

    A those in which things are coming to an end

    B those in which there is a lot of activity

    C those in which people are cleaning or camping

    D those in which people are sad

74 2

75 Which of the following words is *not* a term for a poet?

    A bard

    B sonneteer

    C stanzist

    D versifier

75 2

MARK

COMPREHENSION SUB-TOTAL

Q. 76–85 Short writing task

MARK

Write for 20–30 minutes on *one* of the following. Continue on a separate sheet if you need to.

a) A Deserted Place

b) Noise. What kind of noise do you like? When and where do you like it? Or do you always prefer quiet?
   Discuss the importance of noise and quiet in your life.

c) Describe the scene after a party.

_____

_____

_____

_____

_____

_____

_____

_____

_____

_____

_____

_____

_____

_____

_____

_____

_____

_____

_____

_____

_____

_____

_____

_____

END OF TEST

	MARK
SHORT WRITING TASK SUB-TOTAL	10
English skills sub-total (from page 47)	60
Comprehension sub-total (from page 50)	30
Short writing task sub-total (from this page)	10
PAPER 18 TOTAL MARK	100

Progress chart

Write the score (out of 100) for each paper in the box provided at the bottom of the chart. Then colour in the column above the box to the appropriate height to represent this score.

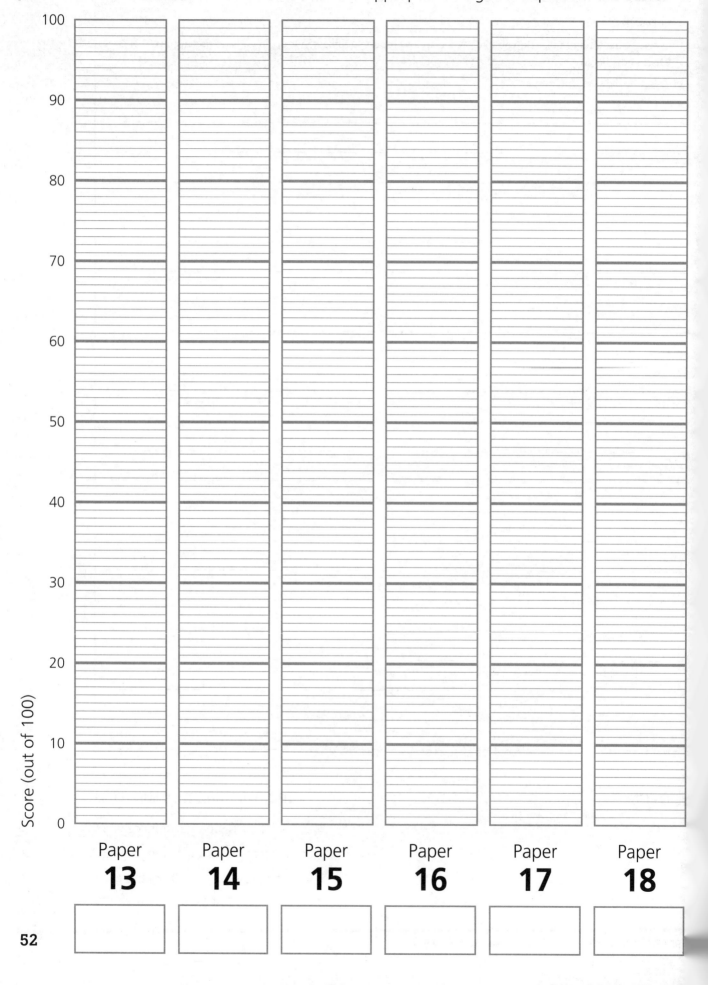

Score (out of 100)

Paper	Paper	Paper	Paper	Paper	Paper
13	**14**	**15**	**16**	**17**	**18**